W9-CPF-681

Read and Do Science

SOLID, LIQUID, and GAS

Written by Melinda Lilly
Photos by Scott M. Thompson
Design by Elizabeth Bender

Educational Consultants

Kimberly Weiner, Ed.D

Betty Carter, Ed.D

Maria Czech, Ph.D
California State University Northridge

Rourke

Publishing LLC

Vero Beach, Florida 32963

Before You Read This Book

1. List ten things that you can see. Do they have anything in common with one another? Can you sort them into groups?

2. The word gas can mean different things, it can even be another name for gasoline. What is the difference between the gas that goes in cars and gases like air? Is gasoline a liquid or a gas?

The experiments in this book should be undertaken with adult supervision.

For Henry

—S. T.

©2004 Rourke Publishing LLC

Library of Congress Cataloging-in-Publication Data

ISBN 1-58952-648-1

Printed in the USA

Table of Contents

How would you describe yourself?

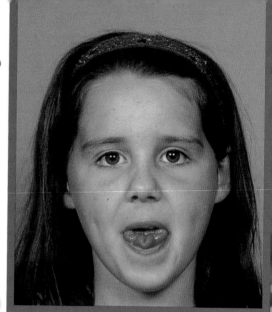

Are you someone who can . . .
Skip? Curl your tongue?
Jump? Swing?

4

How about describing yourself as **matter?** Everything that takes up space is matter, including you.

Scientists sort matter into three groups: **solids, liquids,** and **gases.**

Where do you fit in?

Pat yourself on the back.

Did you make a splash when you patted your back? No? Your back isn't a liquid.

Liquids are wet, can be poured, and have no shape of their own. If you pour water into a pitcher, it will take on the shape of the pitcher. If you pour it on the ground it will puddle.

Does your back feel like a cloud? Does it float and spread out? No? Then your back isn't a gas.

Your back is solid. It is firm and has a shape that changes only with effort.

Now stick out your tongue. Grab it. Is it wet? More than half of your body is made of liquid.

Breathe in and out. Air is a gas. Part of your body is gas.

Sometimes gas comes out as a burp.

People are made of solids, liquids, and gases.

11

Make a goop that can be solid or liquid.

Goop

What You Need:
- 7 cups cornstarch
- 4 cups water
- Drop of food coloring (if you want colored goop)
- Bowl

Pour cornstarch into the bowl.

Add coloring to the water.

Mix the water and cornstarch together.

Poke the goop. It's solid. For a moment it's firm and has shape.

Let it flow. The goop becomes a liquid.

Oh no! They're made of solid, liquid, gas . . . and

goop!

The Mysteries of Goop

When you poke your finger into liquid, the liquid flows out of the way. Things that are solid stay put. That's why no one swims in dirt.

When you poke your finger in goop, the water flows out of the way. What's left is solid cornstarch.

Like all matter, gases take up space. They press against things. Air pressure can push very hard. Wind pushes your hair, kites, and can even push over trees!

The motion for the word "wind," in sign language

Use **air pressure** to do a magic scientific trick!

Amazing Air

What You Need:
- A playing card
- A small jar with a narrow opening that can be easily covered by the card
- Water to fill the jar halfway
- A place that can get wet

Fill the jar halfway with water.

Cover the opening of the jar with the card. Hold it in place.

Tip over the jar. Smoothly lower your hand, taking it off the card.

The card stays up! Why?

When you turn the jar upside down, a tug-of-war begins between air pressure outside and inside the jar. Air pressure outside the jar pushes up against the card. Air pressure inside the jar pushes down on the card.

It's not an even match—there's a little air inside the jar and a lot of air outside. More air outside means more pressure pushing up.

Watch out!

When the card gets soaked, air seeps into the jar. Pressure increases inside. The card falls.

What Matters?

All matter takes up space and presses against other matter. Matter is organized into groups called solids, liquids, and gases. You're made of all three!

Glossary

air pressure (AIR PRESH ur) — the pressing force or power of air

carbon dioxide (KAR bun die OK sied) — A gas that is breathed out by animals and used in photosynthesis by green plants

gases (GAS iz) — matter that will fill a container and can spread apart without end

liquids (LIK widz) — matter that will flow, will take on the shape of a container, and will not spread apart without end

matter (MAT ur) — stuff or substance that takes up space

solids (SOL idz) — matter that is firm and has a shape

Take It Further: Gas Balloon

The gas that you breathe out is called carbon dioxide. Make **carbon dioxide** fill a balloon! Get a 16-ounce (500-mL) plastic bottle, a balloon, a funnel, 1/3 cup vinegar, and two teaspoons of baking soda.

- Use the funnel to pour the baking soda into the balloon.

- Pour the vinegar into the bottle.

- Stretch the balloon over the neck of the bottle.

- Let the baking soda fall from the balloon into the bottle.

- As the vinegar and baking soda mix, they release carbon dioxide. It bubbles and fills the balloon!

Think About It!

1. Look at the list you wrote before you read this book. Which things are solid, which are liquid, and which are gas?

2. If you put a solid ice cube in the sun, what will happen?

3. Which word belongs with which type of matter?

Water	Solid
Ice	Liquid
Steam	Gas

Index